# AT THE FEET OF THE MASTER

When he was a boy Alcyone (J. Krishna-murti) wrote down the precepts for right living contained in this small book. Since then the work has appeared in many editions and has been a source of inspiration and guidance for thousands of people in many lands.

# AT THE FEET OF
# THE MASTER

by
ALCYONE

*This publication made possible with the*
*assistance of the Kern Foundation.*
The Theosophical Publishing House
Wheaton, Ill. / Madras, India / London, England

ISBN: 0-8356-0196-X

# PREFACE

THE privilege is given to me, as an elder, to pen a word of introduction to this little book, the first written by a younger Brother, young in body verily, but not in Soul. The teachings contained in it were given to him by his Master in preparing him for Initiation, and were written down by him from memory — slowly and laboriously, for his English last year was far less fluent than it is now. The greater part is a reproduction of the Master's own words; that which is not such a verbal reproduction is the Master's thought clothed in His pupil's words. Two omitted sentences were supplied by the Master. In two other cases an omitted word has been added. Beyond this, it is entirely Alcyone's own, his first gift to the world.

May it help others as the spoken teachings helped him — such is the hope with which he gives it. But the teaching can only be fruitful if it is *lived,* as he has lived it, since it fell from the Master's lips. If the example be followed as well as the precept, then for the reader, as for the writer, shall the great Portal swing open, and his feet be set on the Path.

Annie Besant.

असतो मा सद्गमय
तमसो मा ज्योतिर्गमय
मृत्योर्माऽमृतङ्गमय

From the unreal lead me to the Real.
From darkness lead me to Light.
From death lead me to Immortality.

# FOREWORD

THESE are not my words; they are the words of the Master who taught me. Without Him I could have done nothing, but through His help I have set my feet upon the Path. You also desire to enter the same Path, so the words which He spoke to me will help you also, if you will obey them. It is not enough to say that they are true and beautiful; a man who wishes to succeed must do exactly what is said. To look at food and say that it is good will not satisfy a starving man; he must put forth his hand and eat. So to hear the Master's words is not enough, you must do what He says, attending to every word, taking every hint. If a hint is not taken, if a word is missed, it is lost forever; for He does not speak twice.

Four qualifications there are for this pathway:

Discrimination

Desirelessness

Good conduct

**Love**

What the Master has said to me on each of these I shall try to tell **you.**

# AT THE FEET OF THE MASTER

## I

THE first of these Qualifications is Discrimination; and this is usually taken as the discrimination between the real and the unreal which leads men to enter the Path. It is this, but it is also much more; and it is to be practiced, not only at the beginning of the Path, but at every step of it every day until the end. You enter the Path because you have learnt that on it alone can be found those things which are worth gaining. Men who do not know, work to gain wealth and power, but these are at most for one life only, and therefore unreal. There are greater things than these — things which are real and lasting; when you have once seen these, you desire those others no more.

In all the world there are only two kinds of people — those who know, and those who do not know; and this knowledge is the thing which matters. What religion a

man holds, to what race he belongs
—these things are not important;
the really important thing is this
knowledge—the knowledge of God's
plan for men. For God has a plan
and that plan is evolution. When
once a man has seen that and really
knows it, he cannot help working
for it and making himself one with
it, because it is so glorious, so
beautiful. So, because he knows,
he is on God's side, standing for
good and resisting evil, working
for evolution and not for selfish-
ness.

If he is on God's side he is one of us, and it does not matter in the least whether he calls himself a Hindu, or a Buddhist, a Christian or a Muhammadan, whether he is an Indian or an Englishman, a China-man or a Russian. Those who are on His side know why they are here and what they should do, and they are trying to do it; all the others do not yet know what they should do, and so they often act foolishly, and try to invent ways for themselves which they think will be pleasant for themselves, not understanding that all are one, and that therefore only what the One wills can ever be really pleasant for any one. They are following the unreal instead of the real. Until they learn to distinguish between these two, they have not ranged themselves on God's side, and so this discrimination is the first step.

But even when the choice is made, you must still remember that of the real and the unreal there are many varieties; and discrimination must still be made between the right and the wrong, the important and the unimportant, the useful and the useless, the true and the false, the selfish and the unselfish.

Between the right and wrong it should not be difficult to choose, for those who wish to follow the Master have already decided to take the right at all costs. But the body and the man are two, and the man's will is not always what the body wishes. When your body wishes something, stop and think whether *you* really wish it. For *you* are God, and you will only what God wills; but you must dig deep down

10

into yourself to find the God within you, and listen to His voice, which is *your* voice. Do not mistake your bodies for yourself — neither the physical body, nor the astral, nor the mental. Each one of them will pretend to be the Self, in order to gain what it wants. But you must know them all, and know yourself as their master.

When there is work that must be done, the physical body wants to rest, to go out walking, to eat and drink; and the man who does not know says to himself: "*I* want to do these things, and I must do them." But the man who knows says: "This that wants it *not* I, and it must wait awhile." Often when there is an opportunity to help some one, the body feels: "How much trouble it will be for me; let some one else do it." But the man replies to his body: "You shall not hinder me in doing good work."

The body is your animal — the horse upon which you ride. Therefore you must treat it well, and take good care of it; you must not overwork it, you must feed it properly on pure food and drink only, and keep it strictly clean always, even from the minutest speck of dirt. For without a perfectly clean and healthy body you cannot do the arduous work of preparation, you cannot bear its ceaseless strain. But it must always be you who control that body, not it that controls you.

The astral body has *its* desires — dozens of them; it wants you to be angry, to say sharp words, to feel jealous, to be greedy for money, to envy other people their possessions, to yield yourself to depression. All these things it wants, and many more, not because it wishes to harm you, but because it likes violent vibrations, and likes to change them constantly. But *you* want none of these things, and therefore you must discriminate between your wants and your body's.

Your mental body wishes to think itself proudly separate, to think much of itself and little of others. Even when you have turned it away from worldly things, it still tries to

14

calculate for self, to make you think of your own progress, instead of thinking of the Master's work and of helping others. When you meditate, it will try to make you think of the many different things which *it* wants instead of the one thing which *you* want. You are not this mind, but it is yours to use; so here again discrimination is necessary. You must watch unceasingly, or you will fail.

Between right and wrong, Occultism knows no compromise. At whatever apparent cost, that which

is right you must do, that which is
wrong you must not do, no matter
what the ignorant may think or say.
You must study deeply the hidden
laws of Nature, and when you know
them arrange your life according to
them, using always reason and
common-sense.

You must discriminate between
the important and the unimportant.
Firm as a rock where right and
wrong are concerned, yield always
to others in things which do not matter. For you must be always gentle
and kindly, reasonable and accom-

modating, leaving to others the same
full liberty which you need for yourself.

Try to see what is worth doing:
and remember that you must not
judge by the size of a thing. A
small thing which is directly useful
in the Master's work is far better
worth doing than a large thing
which, the world would call good.
You must distinguish not only the
useful from the useless, but the
more useful from the less useful.
To feed the poor is a good and noble
and useful work; yet to feed their

souls is nobler and more useful than to feed their bodies. Any rich man can feed the body, but only those who know can feed the soul. If you know, it is your duty to help others to know.

However wise you may be already, on this Path you have much to learn; so much that here also there must be discrimination, and you must think carefully what is worth learning. All knowledge is useful, and one day you will have all knowledge; but while you have only part, take care that it is the most useful part. God is Wisdom as well as Love; and the more wisdom you have the more you can manifest of Him. Study then, but study first that which will most help you to help others. Work patiently at your studies, not that men may think you wise, not even that you may have the happiness of being wise, but because only the wise man can be wisely helpful. However much you wish to help, if you are ignorant you may do more harm than good.

You must distinguish between

truth and falsehood; you must learn to be true all through, in thought and word and deed.

In thought first; and that is not easy, for there are in the world many untrue thoughts, many foolish superstitions, and no one who is enslaved by them can make progress. Therefore you must not hold a thought just because many other people hold it, nor because it has been believed for centuries, nor because it is written in some book which men think sacred; you must think of the matter for yourself, and of you. If a man does something which you think will harm you, or says something which you think applies to you, do not think at once: "He meant to injure me." Most probably he never thought of you at all, for each soul has its own troubles and its thoughts turn chiefly around itself. If a man speak angrily to you, do not think: "He hates me, he wishes to wound me." Probably some one or something else has made him angry, and because he happens to meet you he turns his anger upon you. He is

22

acting foolishly, for all anger is foolish, but you must not therefore think untruly of him.

When you become a pupil of the Master, you may always try the truth of your thought by laying it beside His. For the pupil is one with his Master, and he needs only to put back his thought into the Master's thought to see at once whether it agrees. If it does not, it is wrong, and he changes it instantly, for the Master's thought is perfect, because He knows all. Those who are not yet accepted by Him cannot do quite this; but they may greatly help themselves by stopping often to think: "What would the Master think about this? What would the Master say or do under these circumstances?" For you must never do or say or think what you cannot imagine the Master as doing or saying or thinking.

You must be true in speech too — accurate and without exaggeration. Never attribute motives to another; only his Master knows his thoughts, and he may be acting from reasons which have never entered your when you think you have finally killed it in one of them, it arises in another as strongly as ever. But by degrees you will become so full of thought for the helping of others that there will be no room, no time, for any thought about yourself.

You must discriminate in yet another way. Learn to distinguish the God in everyone and everything, no matter how evil he or it may appear on the surface. You can help your brother through that which you have in common with him, and that is the Divine Life; learn how to arouse that in him, learn how to appeal to that in him; so shall you save your brother from wrong.

## II

THERE are many for whom the Qualification of Desirelessness is a difficult one, for they feel that they *are* their desires — that if their distinctive desires, their likings and dislikings, are taken away from them, there will be no self left. But these are only they who have not seen the Master; in the light of His holy Presence all desire dies, but the desire to be like Him. Yet before you have the happiness of meeting Him face to face, you may attain desirelessness if you will. Discrimination has already shown you that the things which most men desire, such as wealth and power, are not worth having; when this is really felt, not merely said, all desire for them ceases.

Thus far all is simple; it needs only that you should understand. But there are some who forsake the pursuit of earthly aims only in order to gain heaven, or to attain personal liberation from rebirth;

into this error you must not fall. If you have forgotten self altogether, you cannot be thinking when that self should be set free, or what kind of heaven it shall have. Remember that *all* selfish desire binds, however high may be its object, and until you have got rid of it you are not wholly free to devote yourself to the work of the Master.

When all desires for self are gone, there may still be a desire to see the result of your work. If you help anybody, you want to *see* how much you have helped him; perhaps even you want him to see it too, and to be powers; they will come when the Master knows that it is best for you to have them. To force them too soon often brings in its train much trouble; often their possessor is mislead by deceitful nature-spirits, or becomes conceited and thinks he cannot make a mistake; and in any case the time and strength that it takes to gain them might be spent in work for others. They will come in the course of development — they *must* come; and if the Master sees that it would be useful for you to have them sooner, He will tell you how to unfold them safely. Until then, you are better without them.

You must guard, too, against certain small desires which are common in daily life. Never wish to shine, or to appear clever; have no desire to speak. It is well to speak little; better still to say nothing, unless you are quite sure that what you wish to say is true, kind and helpful. Before speaking think carefully whether what you are going to say has those three qualities; if it has not, do not say it.

It is well to get used even now to

thinking carefully before speaking; for when you reach Initiation you must watch every word, lest you should tell what must not be told. Much common talk is unnecessary and foolish; when it is gossip, it is wicked. So be accustomed to listen rather than to talk; do not offer opinions unless directly asked for them. One statement of the Qualifications gives them thus; to know, to dare, to will, and to be silent; and the last of the four is the hardest of them all.

Another common desire which

you must sternly repress is the wish to meddle in other men's business. What another man does or says or believes is no affair of yours, and you must learn to let him absolutely alone. He has full right to free thought and speech and action, so long as he does not interfere with any one else. You yourself claim the freedom to do what you think proper; you must allow the same freedom to him, and when he exercises it you have no right to talk about him.

If you think he is doing wrong,

and you can contrive an opportunity of privately and very politely telling him why you think so, it is possible that you may convince him; but there are many cases in which even that would be an improper interference. On no account must you go and gossip to some third person about the matter, for that is an extremely wicked action.

If you see a case of cruelty to a child or an animal, it is your duty to interfere. If you see any one breaking the law of the country, you should inform the authorities. If

36

you are placed in charge of another person in order to teach him, it may become your duty gently to tell him of his faults. Except in such cases, mind your own business, and learn the virtue of silence.

## III

THE Six points of Conduct which are specially required are given by the Master as:

1. Self-control as to the Mind.
2. Self-control in Action.
3. Tolerance.
4. Cheerfulness.
5. One-pointedness.
6. Confidence.

[I know some of these are often translated differently, as are the names of the Qualifications; but in all cases I am using the names which the Master Himself employed when explaining them to me.]

1. *Self-control as to the Mind.*— The Qualification of Desirelessness shows that the astral body must be controlled; this shows the same thing as to the mental body. It means control of temper, so that you may feel no anger or impatience; of the mind itself, so that the thought may always be calm and unruffled; and (through the mind) of the nerves, so that they may be as little irritable as possible. This last is

difficult, because when you try to prepare yourself for the Path, you cannot help making your body more sensitive, so that its nerves are easily disturbed by a sound or a shock, and feel any pressure acutely; but you must do your best.

The calm mind means also courage, so that you may face without fear the trials and difficulties of the Path; it means also steadiness, so that you may make light of the troubles which come into every one's life, and avoid the incessant worry over little things in which many people spend most of their time. The Master teaches that it does not matter in the least what happens to a man from the outside; sorrows, troubles, sicknesses, losses, — all these must be as nothing to him, and must not be allowed to affect the calmness of his mind. They are the result of past actions, and when they come you must bear them cheerfully, remembering that all evil is transitory, and that your duty is to remain always joyous and serene. They belong to your previous lives, not to this; you cannot

it may be perfectly done; do not let your mind be idle, but keep good thoughts always in the background of it, ready to come forward the moment it is free.

Use your thought-power every day for good purposes; be a force in the direction of evolution. Think each day of some one whom you know to be in sorrow, or suffering, or in need of help, and pour out loving thought upon him.

Hold back your mind from pride, for pride comes only from ignorance. The man who does not know thinks that he is great, that he has done this or that great thing; the wise man knows that only God is great, that all good work is done by God alone.

2. *Self-control in Action.*—If your thought is what it should be, you will have little trouble with your action. Yet remember that, to be useful to mankind, thought must result in action. There must be no laziness, but constant activity in good work. But it must be your *own* duty that you do — not another man's, unless with his permission

and by way of helping him. Leave
every man to do his own work in
his own way; be always ready to
offer help where it is needed, but
*never* interfere. For many people
the most difficult thing in the world
to learn is to mind their own business; but that is exactly what you
must do.

Because you try to take up higher
work, you must not forget your ordinary duties, for until they are
done you are not free for other service. You should undertake no new
worldly duties; but those which you

have already taken upon you, you must perfectly fulfill — all clear and reasonable duties which you yourself recognize, that is, not imaginary duties which others try to impose upon you. If you are to be His, you must do ordinary work better than others, not worse; because you must do that also for His sake.

3. *Tolerance.*—You must feel perfect tolerance for all, and a hearty interest in the beliefs of those of another religion, just as much as in your own. For their religion is a path to the highest, just as yours is.

And to help all, you must understand all.

But in order to gain this perfect tolerance, you must yourself first be free from bigotry and superstition. You must learn that no ceremonies are necessary; else you will think yourself somehow better than those who do not perform them. Yet you must not condemn others who still cling to ceremonies. Let them do as they will; only they must not interfere with you who know the truth — they must not try to force upon you that which you have outgrown.

Make allowance for everything; be kindly towards everything.

Now that your eyes are opened, some of your old beliefs, your old ceremonies, may seem to you absurd, perhaps, indeed, they really are so. Yet though you can no longer take part in them, respect them for the sake of those good souls to whom they are still important. They have their place, they have their use; they are like those double lines which guided you as a child to write straight and evenly, until you learnt to write far better and more freely without them. There was a time when you needed them; but now that time is past.

A great Teacher once wrote: "When I was a child, I spake as a child, I understood as a child, I thought as a child; but when I became a man I put away childish things." Yet he who has forgotten his childhood and lost sympathy with the children is not the man who can teach them or help them. So look kindly, gently, tolerantly upon all; but upon all alike, Buddhist or

Hindu, Jain or Jew, Christian or Muhammadan.

4. *Cheerfulness.*—You must bear your karma cheerfully, whatever it may be, taking it as an honor that suffering comes to you, because it shows that the Lords of Karma think you worth helping. However hard it is, be thankful that it is no worse. Remember that you are of but little use to the Master until your evil karma is worked out, and you are free. By offering yourself to Him, you have asked that your karma may be hurried, and so now

in one or two lives you work through what otherwise might have been spread over a hundred. But in order to make the best out of it, you must bear it cheerfully, gladly.

Yet another point. You must give up all feeling of possession. Karma may take from you the things which you like best—even the people whom you love most. Even then you must be cheerful—ready to part with anything and everything. Often the Master needs to pour out His strength upon others through His servant; He cannot do that if the servant yields to depression. So cheerfulness must be the rule.

5. *One-pointedness.* —The one thing that you must set before you is to do the Master's work. Whatever else may come in your way to do, that at least you must never forget. Yet nothing else *can* come in your way, for all helpful, unselfish work is the Master's work, and you must do it for His sake. And you must give all your attention to each piece as you do it, so that it may be your very best. The same Teacher also wrote: "Whatsoever ye do, do

it *heartily,* as to the Lord, and not unto men." Think how you would do a piece of work if you knew that the Master was coming at once to look at it; just in that way you must do all your work. Those who know most will most know all that that verse means. And there is another like it, much older: "Whatsoever thy hand findeth to do, do it with thy might."

One-pointedness means, too, that nothing shall ever turn you, even for a moment, from the Path upon which you have entered. No temptations,

no worldly pleasures, no worldly
affections even, must ever draw you
aside. For you yourself must become one with the Path; it must be
so much part of your nature that
you follow it without needing to
think of it, and cannot turn aside.
You, the Monad, have decided it; to
break away from it would be to
break away from yourself.

6. *Confidence.*—You must trust
your Master; you must trust yourself. If you have seen the Master,
you will trust Him to the uttermost,
through many lives and deaths. If

you have not yet seen Him, you must still try to realize Him and trust Him, because if you do not, even He cannot help you. Unless there is perfect trust, there cannot be the perfect flow of love and power.

You must trust yourself. You say you know yourself too well? If you feel so, you do *not* know yourself; you know only the weak outer husk, which has fallen often into the mire. But *you* — the real you — you are a spark of God's own fire, and God, who is Almighty, is in you, and because of that there is nothing that you cannot do if you will. Say to yourself: "What man has done, man can do. I am a man, yet also God in man; I can do this thing, and I will." For your will must be like tempered steel, if you would tread the Path.

## IV

OF all the Qualifications, Love is the most important, for if it is strong enough in a man, it forces him to acquire all the rest, and all the rest without it would never be sufficient. Often it is translated as an intense desire for liberation from the round of births and deaths, and for union with God. But to put it in that way sounds selfish, and gives only part of the meaning. It is not so much desire

57

as *will*, resolve, determination. To produce its result, this resolve must fill your whole nature, so as to leave no room for any other feeling. It is indeed the will to be one with God, not in order that you may escape from weariness and suffering, but in order that because of your deep love for Him you may act with Him and as He does. Because He is Love, you, if you would become one with Him, must be filled with perfect unselfishness and love also.

In daily life this means two things; first, that you shall be careful to do no hurt to any living thing; second, that you shall always be watching for an opportunity to help.

First, to do no hurt. Three sins there are which work more harm than all else in the world — gossip, cruelty, and superstition — because they are sins against love. Against these three the man who would fill his heart with the love of God must watch ceaselessly.

See what gossip does. It begins with evil thought, and that in itself is a crime. For in everyone and in everything there is good; in every-

one and in everything there is evil.
Either of these we can strengthen by
thinking of it, and in this way we
can help or hinder evolution; we can
do the will of the Logos or we can
resist Him. If you think of the evil
in another, you are doing at the
same time three wicked things:

(1) You are filling your neighbor-
hood with evil thought instead of
with good thought, and so you are
adding to the sorrow of the world.

(2) If there is in that man the
evil which you think, you are
strengthening it and feeding it; and

so you are making your brother worse instead of better. But generally the evil is not there, and you have only fancied it; and then your wicked thought tempts your brother to do wrong, for if he is not yet perfect you may make him that which you have thought him.

(3) You fill your own mind with evil thoughts instead of good; and so you hinder your own growth, and make yourself, for those who can see, an ugly and painful object instead of a beautiful and lovable one.

Not content with having done all

this harm to himself and to his vic-
tim, the gossip tries with all his
might to make other men partners
in his crime.  Eagerly he tells his
wicked tale to them, hoping that
they will believe it; and then they
join with him in pouring evil
thought upon the poor sufferer.
And this goes on day after day, and
is done not by one man but by thousands.  Do you begin to see how
base, how terrible a sin this is? You
must avoid it altogether.  Never
speak ill of any one; refuse to listen
when any one else speaks ill of

another, but gently say: "Perhaps this is not true, and even if it is, it is kinder not to speak of it."

Then as to cruelty. This is of two kinds, intentional and unintentional. Intentional cruelty is purposely to give pain to another living being; and that is the greatest of all sins — the work of a devil rather than a man. You would say that no man could do such a thing; but men have done it often, and are daily doing it now. The inquisitors did it; many religious people did it in the name of their religion. Vivisectors do it; many schoolmasters do it habitually. All these people try to excuse their brutality by saying that it is the custom; but a crime does not cease to be a crime because many commit it. Karma takes no account of custom; and the karma of cruelty is the most terrible of all. In India at least there can be no excuse for such customs, for the duty of harmlessness is well-known to all. The fate of the cruel must fall also upon all who go out intentionally to kill God's creatures, and call it "sport."

Such things as these you would not do, I know; and for the sake of the love of God, when opportunity offers, you will speak clearly against them. But there is a cruelty in speech as well as in act; and a man who says a word with the intention to wound another is guilty of this crime. That, too, you would not do; but sometimes a careless word does as much harm as a malicious one. So you must be on your guard against unintentional cruelty.

It comes usually from thoughtlessness. A man is so filled with greed and avarice that he never even thinks of the suffering which he causes to others by paying too little, or by half-starving his wife and children. Another thinks only of his own lust, and cares little how many souls and bodies he ruins in satisfying it. Just to save himself a few minutes' trouble, a man does not pay his workmen on the proper day, thinking nothing of the difficulties he brings upon them. So much suffering is caused just by carelessness — by forgetting to think how an action will affect others. But karma never forgets, and it takes no account of the fact that men forget. If you wish to enter the Path, you must think of the consequences of what you do, lest you should be guilty of thoughtless cruelty.

Superstition is another mighty evil, and has caused much terrible cruelty. The man who is a slave to it despises others who are wiser, tries to force them to do as he does. Think of the awful slaughter produced by the superstition that animals should be sacrificed, and by the still more cruel superstition that man needs flesh for food. Think of the treatment which superstition has meted out to the depressed classes in our beloved India, and see in that how this evil quality can breed heartless cruelty even among those who know the duty of brotherhood. Many crimes have men committed in the name of the God of Love, moved by this nightmare of superstition; be very careful therefore that no slightest trace of it remains in you.

These three great crimes you must avoid, for they are fatal to all progress, because they sin against love. But not only must you thus refrain from evil; you must be active in doing good. You must be so filled with the intense desire of service that you are ever on the watch to render it to all around you — not to man alone, but even to animals and plants. You must render it in small things every day, that the habit may be formed, so that you may not miss the rare opportunity when the great thing living plume of fire, raying out upon the world the Divine Love which fills his heart.

The wisdom which enables you to help, the will which directs the wisdom, the love which inspires the will — these are your qualifications. Will, Wisdom and Love are the three aspects of the Logos; and you, who wish to enroll yourselves to serve Him, must show forth these aspects in the world.

Waiting the word of the Master,
Watching the Hidden Light;
Listening to catch His Orders
In the very midst of the fight;

Seeing His slightest signal
Across the heads of the throng;
Hearing His faintest whisper
Above earth's loudest song.